Praise for *Single-Minded Leadership: The Power of Focus and Determination*

The way Mark has woven together family stories with leadership principles creates a compelling narrative that feels both intimate and universally applicable. His father's legacy comes alive on every page.
Kumar R. Parakala | USA National Best-Selling Author, *Lead to Disrupt*

Single-Minded Leadership is an inspiring tribute to values-driven leadership. Ralph Harvey's story demonstrates how faith, integrity, and perseverance create a legacy far greater than business success. A powerful reminder that true leadership begins with character.
Carl Grant III | Author, *How to Live the Abundant Life*

Ralph doesn't shy away from the difficult moments while maintaining hope and optimism. This honest approach makes the lessons more credible and the victories more meaningful.
Tamara Nall | CEO & Founder, The Leading Niche

Ralph Harvey's generosity and conviction changed the course of my career. In my very first weeks as a fundraiser, he pledged a full matching challenge that doubled our goal and launched nearly two decades of impact. He was jovial yet driven, strong yet tender with his family, and he never wavered in his belief that blessings were meant to be poured out on others. This book captures the faithfulness and strength that defined his leadership.
Celia Palmer | Former Executive Director, Cystic Fibrosis Foundation (Central Oklahoma Chapter)

What strikes readers most is how Mark shows leadership as daily choices rather than grand gestures. The quiet moments of integrity and generosity are just as powerful as the business victories.
Shawn Johal | Business Growth Coach, Elevation Leaders, Bestselling Author of *The Happy Leader*

The progression from vision to legacy feels natural and well-crafted, with each chapter building on the last. Mark has created a coherent philosophy of leadership that readers can actually follow.
Trissa Tismal-Capili | USA Today and Wall Street Journal Bestselling Author

It's a heartfelt tribute to a man who led with purpose, grit, and compassion. Through his father's story, Mark brings leadership lessons to life with honesty, humility, and emotional depth. The book is a masterclass in how personal values shape professional excellence. Every chapter reveals not only what it means to lead, but why it matters. Mark doesn't just teach leadership—he honors it.
Carolyne M. Chatel, B.A, (E)MBA | Co Founder WIGUP Corp., Executive VP Développement International Development | Founder U SHINE Movement

SINGLE-MINDED LEADERSHIP

THE POWER OF FOCUS AND DETERMINATION

MARK N. HARVEY, M.D.

Copyright © 2025 Mark N. Harvey, M.D.
Published in the United States by Leaders Press.
www.leaderspress.com

All rights reserved. No part of this book may be reproduced or transmitted in any form or by any means, electronic or mechanical, including photocopying, recording, or by any information storage and retrieval system, except by a reviewer who may quote brief passages in a review to be printed in a magazine or newspaper. The contents of this book may not be used to train large language models or other artificial intelligence products without written permission from the copyright holder.

ISBN 978-1-63735-364-6 (pbk)
ISBN 978-1-63735-365-3 (hcv)
ISBN 978-1-63735-363-9 (ebook)

Library of Congress Control Number: 2025915248

Table of Contents

Foreword vii

Dedication xi

Prologue xiii

Introduction: The Power of a Single-Minded Leader xv

Chapter 1: Unwavering Vision: The Birth of Single-Mindedness 1

Chapter 2: Fanning the Flames: Cultivating Passion and Purpose. 11

Chapter 3: The Power of Conviction: Turning Belief
Into Action 19

Chapter 4: Sustaining the Journey: Resilience and the
Single-Minded Leader 27

Chapter 5: A Beacon for Others: How One Life Can
Light the Way for Many 35

Chapter 6: A Legacy in the Making: The Long-Term Impact of
Determined Leadership 45

Conclusion: A Legacy of Values: Tools for Building a
Life of Purpose and Impact 55

Carrying the Legacy Forward 63

Foreword

Single-Minded Leadership: The Power of Focus and Determination is a book about an extraordinary man, Ralph L. Harvey, written by his loving and admiring son, Dr. Mark Harvey. Ralph L. Harvey, the subject of this book, may have been ordinary in some ways, but in countless others, he was a great man. It is his remarkable greatness that is celebrated in the pages that follow.

Ralph was a self-made man who rose from very humble beginnings to a life of considerable success and impact. His ascent was not due to luck or inheritance, but rather to a laser-like focus and an unyielding determination in everything he pursued. He learned early that effort, endurance, honesty, and discipline would be the cornerstones of his life. Working his way through school at all levels, he ultimately earned a master's degree in geology from the University of Oklahoma. When he entered the oil and gas industry during a period of economic hardship known as an "oil bust," he was laid off from Shell Oil Company through no fault of his own. But Ralph never gave in to setbacks. He overcame every disappointment with confidence in his own abilities and faith in the divine plan he believed guided his life. He believed it was a plan to prosper him, not to harm him (Jeremiah 29:11). Ralph became an oil and gas industry entrepreneur.

Ralph's generosity was evident long before financial success found him. He gave consistently to causes he believed in, and when he became a man of means, his giving grew exponentially. His contributions to churches and schools, particularly those connected to the Church of Christ and to conservative political causes, were substantial and heartfelt. And when two of his beloved grandchildren were diagnosed with cystic fibrosis, Ralph became one of the most generous individual supporters of CF research in the country.

I had the privilege of serving as Ralph's primary legal counsel from 1979 until his retirement. Knowing Ralph changed my professional life. He was a client who became a mentor, a dear friend, and to many of us, a moral compass. Ralph had an extraordinarily logical mind and an exceptional eye for detail. I often joked that he would have made an outstanding attorney. He surprised me one day by revealing that he had taken the Law School Aptitude Test, scored very well, and had enrolled in the University of Oklahoma College of Law. Though he eventually stepped away from school to focus on his business, his year in law school became yet another example of Ralph's restless pursuit of excellence and truth.

Ralph was not a man to stand on the sidelines when he saw wrongdoing. Once he formed an opinion rooted in principle, he acted, regardless of the financial or personal cost. He was not motivated by gain or acclaim but by an unwavering sense of what was right. In many legal and civic matters, his courage and leadership helped shape Oklahoma law and policy in ways that still resonate today.

To those who knew him, Ralph was approachable, loyal, and full of life. He greeted strangers with warmth and treated all people with respect, regardless of status or standing. He had a sharp wit and a contagious laugh. He could take a joke as easily as he could tell one, and he never took himself too seriously. Those people in his sphere of influence admired him not just for his accomplishments, but for his character.

Ralph's leadership was of the rarest kind, the kind that flows not from titles, but from example. He showed others how to persevere. He lived out his values daily. He inspired those around him to be diligent, honest, and kind. He believed in lifting people up, encouraging them to stay the course, and supporting causes worth fighting for. His mantra was simple: no matter what, don't ever give up.

Mark N. Harvey, M.D.

I count it one of the great blessings of my life to have known Ralph Harvey. He made me a better lawyer, and I believe, a better man. The lessons I learned from him endure, as I know they will for all who read this book. Ralph Harvey was a leader worth following, a friend worth treasuring, and a man worth remembering.

—Harry H. Selph, II

Harry Selph has been a trusted advisor and close friend to our family for decades. He worked alongside my father as his attorney, confidant, and sounding board, helping navigate pivotal decisions with clarity and care. My father leaned on Harry's thoughtful guidance in both professional and personal matters, a relationship built on deep trust and mutual respect. Today, Harry continues to be a key advisor to me and our team. His ability to think critically and offer clear, grounded direction has been invaluable to us all.

Dedication

For my father, whose quiet leadership changed lives. And for all those who believe that character still matters.

Ralph and Maxine

Prologue

It was a hot summer day in Oklahoma. The sun beat down hard, and a warm wind swept through our backyard. We lived in a quiet neighborhood filled with family homes, where every yard was kept neat and tidy. Mowing the lawn was my responsibility, along with weeding and cleaning out the flowerbeds. I hated every bit of it, but it wasn't optional. My parents expected me to finish my work and do it well.

Before I could start mowing, I had to clean up after our German Shepherd. I trudged around with a shovel, holding my nose and muttering under my breath. Once I finished, I grabbed the mower and got to work. My father was nearby, working in the flowerbeds as I pushed the rotary mower across the uneven grass.

I didn't notice the fresh pile of poop I had missed. The mower hit it, and the spinning blades flung it directly into my face and mouth. It all happened so fast. First, the awful smell hit me, then the sticky warmth on my cheek, and finally, the disgusting taste. I dropped the mower, stumbled backward, and started yelling and crying. I didn't say any actual words, just loud yelling and a panicked sound like I was in serious danger.

My father came running over. At first, he looked concerned, but when he realized what had happened, he started laughing. It wasn't a small laugh, either. He bent over, holding his stomach, laughing so hard he could barely speak. At first, it made me even more upset, but soon I couldn't help myself. His laugh was so contagious that I started laughing, too, even though I was still crying.

After a moment, he walked me over to the garden hose and helped me rinse off. The cold water felt good, but I couldn't shake the lingering smell and gritty taste in my mouth. I expected him to say something comforting, but instead, he looked at me and said, "Mark, sometimes you just have to eat a little shit, clean yourself up, and keep going."

I didn't fully understand what he meant at the time, but I finished cleaning up and went back to mowing the lawn. That moment stayed with me. His words weren't just about that day. They were about life. When something unexpected and unpleasant happens, you deal with it, clean up, and move forward. It's a lesson I've carried ever since.

Looking back, I realized that my father lived by this philosophy every day. Whether in business or life, he faced obstacles head-on, never letting setbacks define him. That single-minded leadership shaped not only his success but the legacy he left behind.

Leadership lessons aren't always learned in boardrooms or classrooms. Sometimes they come from the messes we least expect. Real resilience begins when we refuse to quit, no matter how humble the circumstances.

Introduction

The Power of a Single-Minded Leader

In today's fast-paced, ever-changing world, leadership is often measured by short-term wins, quick decisions, and fleeting success. But what if the secret to making a lasting impact doesn't come from chasing every opportunity but from focusing on a core set of values that guide every choice? What if true success isn't about quarterly profits but about aligning your actions with your beliefs and building a legacy that endures?

This book is about that kind of leadership. It's about the power of a leader whose success isn't driven by reacting to every whim of the market but by a steadfast commitment to a clear vision, strong values, and an unrelenting determination to make a difference. My father, Ralph Harvey, was that kind of leader, and his journey offers lessons that are even more relevant today.

Why This Book Matters Now

As leaders, we all face moments that test our principles. It's easy to get swept up in the demands of the moment, to compromise on what we believe, or to prioritize short-term gains over long-term success. This book presents a different perspective: the idea that true and lasting success comes from aligning with your core values.

Whether you're leading a business, a team, or a community, the principles in this book are universal. They aren't just strategies; they're the foundation of leadership that creates trust, loyalty, and a lasting legacy. These values help us build organizations that withstand storms that ambition alone cannot weather.

This book is for those who want to make a lasting impact, not just in business but in the lives of people they serve. It's for leaders who believe that success is about more than financial performance—it's about building a legacy of purpose, integrity, and generosity.

The Journey Ahead

This book will take you into the mindset of a single-minded leader through practical principles that shaped my father's life:

- **Vision:** How a clear and compelling vision drives every decision, even in the face of adversity.

- **Resilience:** The importance of bouncing back from setbacks and turning obstacles into opportunities with the right mindset.

- **Passion with Purpose:** How to channel competitive fire toward goals that matter, not just for personal success, but for the greater good.

- **Faith and Generosity:** Why giving and leading with integrity are crucial to building a reputation that stands the test of time.

- **Community and Mentorship:** How surrounding yourself with like-minded people and investing in others' success creates an environment where everyone thrives.

Through real-life stories, including the challenges and triumphs my father faced, you'll gain insights into leadership techniques that you can apply to your own life and work.

Values-First Leadership

At the heart of this book is the belief that values alignment is the key to true success. My father's leadership was built on his ability to stay true to his principles, even when the easier path would have been to compromise. His success didn't come from chasing trends or making decisions based on what was convenient; it came from his unwavering commitment to what he believed in.

For our family, values come first, always—in business, philanthropy, and life. We believe that aligning ourselves with people and organizations that share our values is the most important factor in creating lasting success. This book is an invitation to reflect on your own values and explore how aligning them with your leadership can lead to the kind of success that endures.

An Invitation to Collaborate

For those who seek to collaborate with us, whether as advisors, partners, or fellow leaders, this book serves as an introduction to the values that drive everything we do. We are a values-first family, and we believe that true success comes from working with people who share our vision.

The lessons in this book are not just theories. They're lived experiences that have shaped who we are and how we lead. As the next-generation leader in my family, I've embraced these values as my own, and they guide every decision we make, both in business and philanthropy. Our mission is to continue this legacy, and we hope this book inspires you to do the same.

Leadership is about building something that outlives you. Let's build it with vision, resilience, faith, and heart.

Chapter 1
Unwavering Vision: The Birth of Single-Mindedness

"Vision is the art of seeing what is invisible to others."
—Jonathan Swift

From the very beginning, my father stood out because of his extraordinary ability to see what others could not. Where most saw only obstacles, he saw possibilities. His capacity to visualize success long before it materialized became a defining trait that would guide his entire life and career.

Ralph at home after a day of work as a roughneck in the oil field. At the time, he was also a college student.

Inspired by His Father's Entrepreneurialism

The earliest seeds of my father's vision were planted by his father, my grandfather Opel Harvey. A welder who took on backbreaking work in the oilfields of Oklahoma, my grandfather never backed down from a challenge. I can still hear my father recalling the long hours his father spent in the blazing heat, welding large metal tanks with precision and patience.

"My father taught me that it's not enough just to start something," he would say. "You have to see it through, no matter what."

Those early lessons weren't just about hard work; they were about commitment, grit, and integrity. My father observed that success required more than simply putting in the hours—it demanded doing the work with pride regardless of hardship. That sense of purpose would become the foundation of his entrepreneurial spirit.

Driven to Build His Own Business

As he grew older, my father became determined to build something of his own. He wasn't content with just making a living. He wanted to create a lasting impact, a legacy that would outlive him. Inspired by his father's work ethic and driven by his own vision, he set his sights on entrepreneurship.

What fueled him was more than ambition; it was a deep desire to create stability and opportunity for his family. The oil industry, known for its volatility, held immense potential, but my father wasn't just focused on weathering its ups and downs. He wanted to thrive in it by building something lasting. He often shared how a move to California during World War II shaped his understanding of opportunity. Watching his parents step up and contribute to the war effort taught him that every role, no matter how small, can have a lasting impact. That lesson became one of the guiding principles in his life.

When work dried up in Oklahoma during World War II, my grandfather had to find another way to provide for his family. He and my grandmother packed up their lives and moved to California, where jobs were available in the shipyards. Building ships for the war effort gave him steady work, but it also meant a complete change for their family.

My grandfather knew they would need all the help they could get, so he taught my grandmother how to weld. She worked right alongside him in the shipyards, contributing to the war effort in a way she never expected. After the war ended, my grandmother never welded again. But during that time, they both played an important role in something much bigger than themselves.

For my father, watching his parents contribute to the war effort as welders taught him a powerful lesson. He realized that even the smallest contributions could create a ripple effect, touching the lives of many. That understanding became a guiding principle in his life and career: leadership wasn't just about the outcome; it was about the impact. He understood that success isn't achieved by one person alone, but by people working together, each doing their part with integrity and purpose.

I believe that seed was planted during those years in the shipyards. My father saw firsthand that you don't have to lead the entire mission to make a difference. You just have to show up, do your part, and follow through on your responsibilities. That understanding shaped the way he led his business, his family, and his life.

Every great endeavor begins with a personal why. A drive larger than personal gain.

Fighting Forward

A boxing match from Ralph's college days

Long before he stepped into a boardroom or drilled his first successful oil well, my father learned how to fight—not just with his fists, but with his heart, mind, and spirit.

He grew up surrounded by oilfield tanks and meatpacking plants, where toughness wasn't just respected; it was expected. His father's message was simple: "Do what you say. Finish what you start." His mother's motto was equally direct: "Buckle down or buckle under." By age 14, he had turned the local park into his training ground, where neighborhood boys gathered to spar and emulate their boxing heroes.

For my father, boxing wasn't merely a sport; it was a laboratory for developing discipline and focus. Every jab, slip, and counterpunch required calculation and control—skills that would later define his approach to business challenges. In the ring, he discovered that raw talent mattered less than persistence, strategy, and the willingness to absorb punishment without losing heart.

This early passion followed him to college, where his days became a testament to his growing work ethic. He would rise before dawn for shifts as a roughneck on drilling rigs, his hands raw and body aching from the physical demands. Between these grueling shifts, he attended classes, studying the scientific principles behind the oil he was working to extract. Then at night, he would lace up his gloves and step into the gym, where his world narrowed to footwork, head movement, and the rhythmic sound of punches landing against leather.

What began as a pastime evolved into serious competition when he discovered the Golden Gloves tournament. The regional matches drew talented fighters from across the Southwest, many with formal training and established pedigrees. My father had neither—just natural ability, a relentless work ethic, and the hunger to test himself against the best.

His approach to boxing mirrored how he would later tackle business challenges. He studied opponents carefully, identifying patterns and weaknesses. He maintained rigorous conditioning so he could outlast rivals in later rounds. Most importantly, he developed the mental toughness to absorb setbacks without losing focus on his ultimate goal.

The tournament circuit proved challenging but rewarding. After winning at the local level, he advanced to regional competitions where the skill level increased dramatically. Other boxers often came from established programs with professional coaches, while my father was largely self-taught, piecing together techniques from observation and natural instinct.

The Southwest Regional Championship became his defining moment as a boxer. In the semifinal match, he faced a heavily favored opponent with significantly more experience. The fight was brutal, with my father absorbing punishment in the early rounds. But he had developed extraordinary stamina through his oilfield work, and as his opponent tired in the later rounds, my father's relentless pressure began to turn the tide.

In the final round, bloodied but unbowed, he landed a devastating combination that sent his opponent's mouthguard flying—a moment captured in the photograph that he kept throughout his life. The victory qualified him for the National Championship, the pinnacle of amateur boxing and a potential stepping stone to Olympic competition.

Yet despite this triumph, his journey in boxing would end here. The financial reality of traveling to nationals while maintaining his college studies and work schedule proved impossible. Without hesitation, he made the difficult decision to hang up his gloves and refocus on his education and career.

What's remarkable is that he made this choice without regret or bitterness. He had proven himself in the ring, and now it was time to apply those same qualities—discipline, strategic thinking, resilience, and adaptability—to new challenges. The lessons of boxing became permanent fixtures in his approach to life:

- **Discipline:** Split knuckles taught him to keep pushing forward through pain.

- **Adaptation:** Facing taller opponents forced him to adjust his strategy, just as market shifts would require flexibility years later.

- **Resolve:** "In the ring," he'd say, "you don't quit. You breathe through busted ribs and keep moving."

He never stood on a national stage with his gloves raised in victory, but the spirit of the fighter never left him. Every time he faced a business setback, confronted a legal challenge, or navigated a market downturn, he drew upon the same resilience that had carried him through those championship bouts. The ring had taught him that victory isn't always found in trophies or recognition, but in the invisible strength forged through struggle.

Grit is grown long before goals are achieved. It's built in the hidden moments where no one else is looking.

This is one of my favorite pictures of my father in a Golden Gloves tournament. You can see his opponent's mouth guard flying out as he knocked him out. He was in college at the time, boxing in the early 1950s.

Never Giving Up Despite Early Failures

Failure became a frequent companion in my father's early entrepreneurial efforts. Like many who chase ambitious dreams, he encountered numerous setbacks: contracts fell through, ventures collapsed, and often the path forward seemed impossibly steep. Yet through it all, he refused to surrender.

"It's not the fall that defines you," he would often say. "It's the decision to get back up." For him, every failure represented an opportunity to learn, refine his approach, and return stronger. The volatile oil industry became his proving ground, testing and strengthening his resolve with each challenge.

Even when odds seemed insurmountable, he held firm in his belief that perseverance would eventually yield results. He understood that entrepreneurship wasn't about avoiding failure but learning from it to build greater resilience. Each setback taught him something valuable that would inform his next attempt, gradually building the experience and wisdom that would later define his success.

Resilience is the decision to believe in your vision even when circumstances tempt you to walk away.

Visualizing Future Success

One of my father's most extraordinary traits was his ability to envision success well before it materialized. He possessed a rare gift for seeing beyond immediate struggles to focus on the bigger picture. Where others saw risk, he recognized opportunity. Where others hesitated, he moved forward with conviction.

This visionary mindset took root early in his life, long before he entered the oil industry. As a young boy, he would ride the trolley car to the local hospital, carrying leftover newspapers from his father's delivery route to sell to patients and visitors.

During one of these visits, a chance conversation changed the trajectory of his life. A patient asked what he wanted to be when he grew up. Already drawn to the oil business, my father confidently replied that he wanted to become a petroleum engineer.

The patient listened thoughtfully before offering advice that would prove transformative: "You should be a geologist instead. The geologist is the one who finds the oil. The engineer just gets it out of the ground."

That simple observation resonated deeply with my father. From that moment, his vision crystallized. He wasn't interested in managing what others discovered—he wanted to be the one making the discoveries. This clarity of purpose drove him through his education, early career struggles, and eventually to success in the oil industry.

This mindset wasn't about taking blind chances. It involved calculating risks, planning meticulously, and trusting that disciplined effort would produce the results he envisioned. This combination of clear vision and unwavering self-belief propelled him through every challenge he faced throughout his life.

True leadership is the art of seeing what could be and committing to building it before anyone else believes it's possible.

Conclusion: The Birth of a Single-Minded Leader

Looking back on my father's life, it's clear that his determined approach wasn't innate—it was cultivated through formative experiences, hard-won lessons, and the unwavering vision he maintained. From his early influences at home to the discipline of the boxing ring and the unpredictable challenges of the oil industry, he developed a resilience and focus that defined his leadership.

His capacity to remain true to his vision regardless of obstacles became his defining characteristic. His story demonstrates that authentic leadership isn't about avoiding failure but embracing it as an essential part of growth. With vision, grit, and resilience, he proved that seemingly insurmountable challenges could become stepping stones to greater achievements.

Vision alone dreams. Single-minded perseverance builds.

Chapter 2

Fanning the Flames: Cultivating Passion and Purpose

*"Success is the sum of small efforts,
repeated day in and day out."*
—Robert Collier

Racing to Be Out Front

From an early age, my father's competitive spirit burned brightly. One of my earliest memories of this fire was him challenging the high school athletes in the Sunday School class he taught to foot races. It wasn't just about getting there. It was about getting there first. Those races weren't just a fun way to connect with his students; they were a metaphor for how he approached every challenge in life. He didn't just participate. He pushed himself to be out in front, to go beyond what others expected.

This relentless drive to be the best translated into his career as well. Whether navigating the tumultuous oil industry or fighting for business opportunities that others might shy away from, my father treated each new challenge like a race. It was about more than just competing. It was about strategy, preparation, and the sheer will to succeed. That passion for pushing boundaries and striving for excellence became the foundation of his leadership style, influencing every decision he made and every goal he set.

Passion without effort fades. Purpose without competition never stretches its full strength.

Playing "Win at All Costs" Baseball

Despite my father's competitive nature, he knew that winning was not instant and had to be built over time. Sports, especially baseball, gave my father another outlet for his competitive nature. He didn't just play for fun. He played to win, and he expected the same from those around him. As my youth baseball coach, he passed that mentality on to every player he worked with, teaching them that the game wasn't just about athleticism. It was about resilience, teamwork, and pushing yourself to be better, even when the odds were against you.

Our first year as a team was anything but polished. Despite my father's competitive nature, he knew that winning wasn't immediate—it had to be built. We were a group of beginners with no baseball experience, and most of us ended up together because the other teams had already picked the more athletic and experienced eight-year-olds. Many of us didn't know how to throw or catch, let alone play the game.

My father worked with each of us individually, teaching us the basics with patience and encouragement. He celebrated every small improvement and kept us motivated, even when we weren't winning games. At the end of the season, we had a mother-son baseball game to celebrate. It was a humbling experience. Our moms, with their surprising athletic talent, beat us handily. We joked that we could see the future success of some of the team reflected in their moms' skills. Looking back, that season wasn't about the number of wins. It was about being taught, encouraged, and finding joy in the game.

This is my father's high school football picture. He attended Classen High School in Oklahoma City, Oklahoma.

One of the lessons I'll never forget is how he never let a loss pass without reflection. After each game, whether it was a win or a loss, he'd gather the team and go over every play, asking what they could have done differently and how they could better prepare next time. For my father, success wasn't just about the scoreboard. Success was about growth and improvement. The discipline he cultivated in those young athletes mirrored the discipline he applied in his business, where he constantly refined his approach, learned from setbacks, and never stopped striving to be better.

True winning isn't about the scoreboard; it's about building the kind of character that can carry success with humility.

Teaching Bible Classes

Faith wasn't something my father kept separate from his work or his everyday life. Faith was the foundation of everything he did. One of the most significant ways he expressed that faith was by teaching Bible classes. These weren't just lessons in scripture. They were lessons in life, integrity, and the importance of living by your values.

He believed deeply in the timeless truths found in the Bible and took great pride in helping young people navigate their spiritual journeys. But my father didn't just teach these lessons. He lived by these principles in every action. The principles he taught shaped every decision he made, whether in business or in personal relationships. Teaching Bible classes wasn't just about imparting knowledge. It was about sharing his heart, his belief in the power of faith, and the values that had guided him through life's challenges.

I have copies of notes my father wrote while planning classes for young adults. Pages filled with crossed-out ideas, questions to ask students, and outlines for activities. At first glance, his classes seemed spontaneous, full of jokes, shared meals, and games. But his notes show how carefully he prepared. He'd write phrases like, "Emphasize follow-through" or "Ask about their goals first, then connect to responsibility."

He spent hours studying, reading, and planning what he would teach and share with others. In college, he'd pull ideas from books or conversations with coworkers. He believed his words could change lives, so he weighed them carefully. Before discussing a topic like gratitude, he'd ask himself: "Is this true? Have I lived it?"

Though he came across as easygoing, he took his role seriously. He knew students might remember a single comment for years. His approach blended his faith, a commitment to service, and the practicality he'd learned growing up in a working-class home. Stories about keeping promises or helping others weren't just lessons. They were his own rules.

The classes became his life's road map. Teaching others to work hard, give everything, and stay grateful reinforced those values in his own life. Even the fun moments had a purpose. A group hike wasn't just a hike; it was a way to show that responsibility could include joy.

Years later, former students wrote to him. One said, "You made me believe I could rebuild after failing." That was the point. He didn't want to lecture. He wanted to live what he taught, one planned word, one shared meal, at a time.

Real leadership isn't just spoken; it's lived out. Your life becomes your greatest lesson.

Giving Significantly

For my father, giving wasn't a duty; it was a privilege, a natural extension of his faith. He believed that everything he earned was a blessing from God, and he felt a deep responsibility to use those blessings to help others. His generosity wasn't about portioning out a little here and there. He often gave everything he had, driven by a desire to make a real and lasting impact on the lives of those around him.

Giving, for him, wasn't just about money; it was about investing in people, meaningful causes, and the future. His belief in stewardship showed in the thoughtful way he gave. He didn't just write checks. He carefully considered where his resources could do the most good, ensuring that his contributions would continue to make a difference long after they were made. Whether he was supporting a local church, funding educational opportunities, or helping someone in need, my father's generosity was always purposeful, guided by faith and his deep sense of responsibility to improve the lives of others.

My father didn't believe in giving a set percentage of his income as a way to meet a requirement. He saw tithing as a routine obligation for many, a box to check. But to him, true generosity was something deeper. He never thought of himself as "giving back" because he believed that everything he had already belonged to God. His role was to put it to use, grow it, and make an impact on the people around him.

He had an unshakable belief that God would always provide. To him, wealth and resources weren't meant to be stored away. They were meant to be invested, expanded, and used to do good. In the Bible, the Parable of the Talents illustrates two kinds of people—those who hide what they have and those who multiply it. From as early as I can remember, my father believed his duty was clear: multiply everything.

One of his college friends once shared a story that showed how deeply this belief shaped him. Their school had daily chapel services, and one day, a member of a well-known family foundation spoke. That family had made a large donation to fund a new building on campus. My father was sitting next to my mother, who was his girlfriend at the time. His friend, sitting behind them, overheard my father lean over and whisper to her, "Someday, I'm going to do that."

That wasn't a wish or a hope. It was a certainty. He trusted that God would bless him with the ability to give in a way that made a real difference. Looking back over his life, I can see the many times that belief was proven right. He didn't just hold onto what he had—he invested it, multiplied it, and made sure it created a lasting impact.

Generosity isn't about what we give up; it's about what we build up in others.

Surrounding Himself with Believers and Doers

My father had a unique ability to attract like-minded people, individuals who shared his values and his passion for making a difference. He believed that the people you surround yourself with shape who you become, and he was intentional about building a network of believers and doers. These weren't just people who talked about making a difference. They were people who lived it, day in and day out.

Throughout his life, my father surrounded himself with individuals driven by purpose and guided by faith. Whether in business or his personal life, he sought out those who believed in something greater than themselves and who were committed to turning their beliefs into action. His closest friends and colleagues weren't just his support system; they were his inspiration. They challenged him to be better, to stay true to his values, and to continue striving for excellence in everything he did.

He built lifelong friendships and kept them strong. Even as he got older, he stayed connected with friends from his early years, college, his first jobs, and his church. When he met someone whose values aligned with his, that bond lasted. He surrounded himself with people of action, faith, and purpose, and their shared commitment to making a difference fueled his own drive. Many of them went on to create lasting impact in their own ways. If someone's values didn't align with his, he didn't dwell on it. He simply kept moving forward with those who did. The community of believers and doers he built wasn't just about mutual success—it was about creating a legacy of positive impact. Together, they worked to uplift others, support meaningful causes, and live out their faith in tangible ways. One of the most enduring aspects of my father's leadership was his ability to bring together such a dynamic and dedicated group of people, and it remains one of the keys to his success.

We become like the people we surround ourselves with. Choose wisely; your community shapes your future.

Conclusion: Fueling Passion with Purpose

In every part of his life, my father's passion was fueled by a deep sense of purpose. Whether it was his competitive spirit, his faith, or the community of like-minded individuals he cultivated, he lived with a relentless commitment to making a difference. His story is a testament to the power of passion when it's guided by purpose. How a life lived with intention and integrity can inspire others, create lasting change, and leave behind a legacy that endures long after we're gone.

Passion can ignite. Purpose gives it direction. Together, they change lives.

Chapter 3

The Power of Conviction: Turning Belief Into Action

"Conviction is worthless unless it is converted into conduct."
—Thomas Carlyle

Modeling the Work Ethic He Demanded

From the moment my father took on his first job, he believed leadership was built on example. He wasn't the type to simply give orders; he demonstrated what he expected from others by doing the hard work himself. His desk wasn't just where he strategized; it was where he rolled up his sleeves and led by action. Long after others had gone home, he would still be there, working late into the night or starting early in the morning, showing his employees what commitment looked like.

I vividly remember seeing him sit at his desk in the middle of our family room, juggling conversations with us while diligently attending to work matters. It wasn't about balancing work and life for him; it was about bringing the same work ethic into every part of life, whether it was managing a company or keeping things in order at home. He led by example in everything he did, and he expected the same dedication from those around him.

True leadership begins by living the standards you ask of others. The most powerful influence comes from quiet, steady example.

Living His Values Outwardly

For my father, values weren't abstract ideals. They were the core principles that shaped every decision he made, no matter how tough. Integrity, honesty, and responsibility were more than just words to him. Values were the foundation of his leadership. Whenever he faced adversity, he didn't take shortcuts or make excuses. He saw challenges as opportunities to demonstrate accountability, even when the cost was personal.

One of the most powerful examples of this happened when my father was introduced to a young leader who had been referred by someone he trusted. The young man had earned a reputation for success, and my father admired his potential. He seemed to be building a promising business, inspiring others with his drive and ambition. Believing in his promise, my father invited him to take on a leadership role in a new company he had founded.

At first, things seemed to be moving in the right direction. The company was growing, and the young leader appeared to be living up to the high expectations placed on him. But my father, always sharp and observant, started noticing discrepancies. Financial issues were emerging, and the company's success began to falter. It didn't take long for the truth to come out: the young leader was stealing from the company for personal gain.

Confronting this kind of betrayal would shake anyone. But my father, staying true to his values, handled the situation in his own way. When he confronted the young man, he didn't deny it. He admitted to everything. Most people would have cut their losses right then, but not my father. He believed in redemption and gave the man an opportunity to make things right. He offered him a chance to repay the stolen money and work to rebuild the company's finances, extending his guidance and support along the way.

But the young man chose a different path. Instead of taking the chance for redemption, he walked away. He abandoned both the company and the trust my father had placed in him. Despite this bitter outcome, my father held firm. He knew he had acted with integrity, offering a second chance when most wouldn't have. He remained steadfast in his values, believing that doing the right thing wasn't just for when it was easy but especially when it was difficult.

Integrity isn't proven when things are easy. It's revealed when we choose what's right over what's easy, even when it costs us.

Choosing People over Profit

Another powerful example of my father's character came during a particularly tough time for his business. The company was barely holding on financially, with no money in the bank to invest in new oil and gas prospects. The only funds they had left were $50,000, money they desperately needed to keep the business afloat.

Then, a devastating tornado hit Wichita Falls, Texas, leaving a trail of destruction.

When my father heard about the damage, he felt an immediate need to help. Without hesitation, he reached out to a friend involved with a local church and donated the entire $50,000 to assist those in need. His employees were stunned. How could he give away the only money the company had when it was already on shaky ground? Yet, to him, the decision was clear. He was focused on the people who had lost everything.

This wasn't just generosity. It was a sacrifice.

Through this, he taught a powerful lesson: money is a tool, a resource meant to be put to good use when people need it most. At that moment, it wasn't about the survival of his business. It was about the people suffering from the tornado's devastation. For my father, wealth was never meant to be hoarded; it was meant to be shared, especially in times of crisis. His willingness to act without hesitation inspired everyone around him and reinforced what he had always believed: success comes from taking care of people first.

His act of generosity wasn't about getting recognition or praise. It was rooted in his conviction that giving with an open heart would eventually lead to new opportunities. He wasn't worried about how the company would recover without that money. He trusted that another opportunity would come. Throughout his life, my father often gave all he had, believing firmly that something good was always just around the corner.

This moment shaped his perspective on security. From that moment forward, he no longer relied on safety nets. He also trusted his own ability to create success through hard work and perseverance. His company survived and eventually grew into Marlin Oil, the business he had always dreamed of.

But this was not a one-time gesture. My father's life was filled with moments where he gave selflessly, putting others' needs before his own, even when it seemed risky. Generosity wasn't something he did out of convenience—it was a guiding principle that shaped his decisions both in business and in life.

The success he built allowed him to invest not only in oil and gas but also in the lives of those around him—his family, friends, and community.

He showed that the greatest investment we can make is in others.

Supporting Employees in Need

His generosity didn't stop at public donations. It extended to the people who worked for him. I remember one situation in particular when one of his employees faced a devastating personal crisis. Her son was wrongfully accused of a crime after his estranged father falsely claimed he had stolen a car. The legal battle that followed threatened to ruin the boy's future.

My father didn't hesitate. He hired lawyers, paid for investigators, and used every resource at his disposal to clear the boy's name. For him, this wasn't just about saving one young life—it was about standing by his employees and their families when they needed him most. His generosity wasn't a one-time act; it was a daily expression of the values that defined him.

Thanks to his relentless support, the truth finally came to light. All charges were dropped, and the boy's record was cleared. My father's actions not only gave that family their future back but also demonstrated his unwavering commitment to doing what was right, no matter the cost. He showed us that true generosity extends far beyond financial aid. Generosity is about being there for people when it matters most.

Quiet acts of generosity often build more loyalty, hope, and future than the loudest public gestures.

His Quiet Generosity

His generosity wasn't just about responding to emergencies; it was woven into the way he cared for the people in his life. He had a great way of recognizing when someone needed help—and stepping in without hesitation.

My father didn't just show up when things fell apart. He showed up before that. He had a quiet way of noticing when someone was struggling, even if they hadn't said a word. And when he did, he acted. Not for recognition. Not to be admired. Just because that's who he was.

One of the people he helped was a young employee. He'd been hired early in my father's business, back when the young man was still working in banking. The connection ran deeper than work. His wife had been a family friend for years. Her parents were close with mine, the kind of people who show up for each other over time.

The couple had just welcomed their first child, and even with two incomes, they were barely staying afloat. She was a teacher and loved it, but it became clear that what their family really needed was for her to be home with the baby. The math didn't work. And they didn't see a way out.

I don't know if he ever asked my father for help. He probably didn't. But my father found out. Maybe through a friend. Maybe through a conversation someone else had forgotten they even had. He always seemed to know when someone was quietly hurting.

So one day, he pulled the young man into his office and said something simple: "I'm excited for you. I know this baby changes everything. And I know it might be hard to make it work if your wife wants to stay home. I want to help."

Then he gave him a raise. A real one. Big enough that she could stay home with their child, and they could breathe a little easier.

Years later, she told me that moment changed everything. Not just financially. Emotionally. It let them move from surviving to parenting. It gave them margin. And in that margin, they built a life. More kids. More growth. More stability.

That story stuck with me. Because it wasn't just about money. It was about how my father saw people. He didn't just see an employee. He saw a husband trying to do right by his family. He saw a mother trying to show up fully for her child. He saw the whole picture, and he stepped in.

My parents had lived through their own version of that season. Two little kids. Not enough money. Late nights wondering how it was all going to hold together. So when he saw someone else in that same place, he didn't need to be convinced. He just acted.

That's what I remember most. Not just what he gave, but how he gave it. Without fanfare. Without waiting to be asked. And always with an eye toward helping people become who they were meant to be.

True generosity sees what isn't said aloud. It steps in before the need is even voiced. And sometimes, belief comes in the form of a paycheck that makes it possible to stay home with your newborn.

Unwavering Commitment to His Vision

Conviction is not forged in one big decision. It is built daily, in steady choices that stay true to a larger purpose.

My father's generosity went beyond financial aid or personal support. His vision was driven by a desire to create a better future for everyone around him. One of the clearest examples of this was his commitment to education. Despite not having the money at the time, he pledged $2 million to help build a business school and a center for free enterprise at a local university.

He believed deeply in the power of education and free enterprise, confident that his investment would help shape the future for countless students. For him, this pledge wasn't just about money but about creating a legacy of opportunity for generations to come.

Although he was uncomfortable with the attention, seeing his name engraved on the business school's building gave him a quiet sense of pride. That building wasn't just a testament to his success but a symbol of his unwavering commitment to creating a better world through education and opportunity.

This picture was taken during the early years of Marlin Oil, following the successful launch of the business.

Conclusion: Conviction in Action

Reflecting on my father's life, I'm struck by how every action he took was in alignment with his convictions. Whether through small everyday moments or grand gestures of generosity, he never wavered in his belief that hard work, integrity, and generosity could truly change the world.

His legacy isn't just in the buildings that bear his name or the people whose lives he touched through his generosity. It's in the example he set. The power of conviction turned into action. My father's story reminds us all that authentic leadership comes from standing firm in what you believe and living those beliefs every single day.

Conviction without action is just an idea. Conviction lived out builds a legacy.

Chapter 4

Sustaining the Journey: Resilience and the Single-Minded Leader

> *"Success is not final, failure is not fatal: it is the courage to continue that counts."*
> —Winston Churchill

The Crucible of Business Challenges

Resilience isn't forged in moments of comfort; it's shaped in the fires of adversity. My father's journey into entrepreneurship was marked by repeated tests of his determination. In the early days, his first company struggled to gain traction as oil prices fluctuated, contracts fell through, and investors pulled out. What kept him going wasn't luck or outside help—it was his unshakable belief in his ability to succeed.

He never saw failure as the end but as a necessary part of the journey. Each obstacle was a lesson that brought him closer to his goals. "If you're not failing," he often said, "you're not pushing hard enough. Failure is the price you pay for progress."

This resilience was tested most dramatically when the First National Bank of Oklahoma City failed in 1986. The collapse sent shockwaves through the state's business community. My father had built a long-standing relationship with this institution, relying on their support through the volatility of the oil and gas industry. When the collapse came, federal regulators summoned him to San Francisco with a cold directive: pay the debt in full, liquidate assets, or lose everything.

The expectation was that he would dismantle what he had built and walk away with nothing. But my father refused to surrender. After listening carefully to their demands, he offered a counter: if they forced immediate payment, he would declare bankruptcy, and they would recover nothing. If they allowed him to negotiate a structured payment plan, he would honor every cent of his obligation.

They agreed, and he kept his word, settling the debt and saving his business through sheer determination. But he didn't stop there. Across Oklahoma, other families were being crushed by similar situations—not through personal failure but through systemic breakdown. My father began sharing his story with lawmakers, advocating for reforms that would protect future business owners from similar crises.

His advocacy led to meaningful change, including legislation like the Family Wealth Preservation Trust Act and improvements to LLC protections that gave families across the state better tools to weather economic downturns. This experience profoundly shaped his approach to business going forward.

Years later, when presented with an opportunity to take Marlin Oil public, he declined despite the promise of greater capital and expansion. He remembered what it felt like to lose control, to be at the mercy of others' decisions. He chose ownership over scale, stewardship over expansion, protecting his freedom to lead with conviction, even when the cost was high.

True resilience is born when failure is seen not as an end, but as preparation for greater strength.

Competing Through Innovation

My father had a rare gift for seeing possibilities where others saw only limitations. As the industry changed and larger competitors entered the market, he developed a distinctive approach to exploration that became his competitive advantage. He could visualize rock formations and recognize where oil and gas deposits might be found in ways others couldn't perceive.

While studying maps and well data, he would spot patterns that most geologists missed. Over time, he developed personal insights that he treated almost like trade secrets. He often shared these ideas with his petroleum engineer, engaging in spirited debates about unexplored possibilities that challenged conventional thinking.

As energy prices became increasingly unpredictable, he shifted his strategy. Instead of relying on outside investors, he began funding his own exploration projects. He turned his attention to wells that had been deemed unproductive by others. While most in the industry focused on single productive layers of rock, my father looked deeper, examining formations that had been overlooked.

He would attend auctions with carefully researched lists of properties—wells that larger companies had abandoned. After purchasing them, he would work with his team to analyze the geology again, often discovering untapped reserves in places others had written off. This approach allowed him to compete against companies with far greater resources, not by outspending them, but by outthinking them.

Even when this strategy became more challenging in his later years, he remained committed to it. The thrill of finding value where others saw none continued to drive him. It wasn't just about business success—it was about the joy of discovery and the satisfaction of proving that opportunities still existed for those willing to see differently.

True competitive advantage doesn't come from size or wealth. It comes from seeing possibilities others miss.

Maintaining Optimism During Industry Downturns

In the cyclical oil industry, downturns are inevitable. My father faced numerous market collapses that threatened everything he had built, yet he maintained an unwavering optimism grounded in reality. His positive outlook wasn't blind faith—it was a strategic choice based on his understanding that every downturn eventually gives way to recovery.

During the oil price crash of the 1980s, when many companies folded under pressure, my father stayed the course. He made tough but strategic decisions, cutting unnecessary costs while preserving his core team. "Tough times don't last," he would say, "but tough people do." His positivity wasn't just about personal hope—it was about instilling confidence in his employees that together they could weather any storm.

This optimism stemmed from a deep self-awareness. From a young age, he had deliberately chosen to be trustworthy, optimistic, and confident. He understood the uncertainties of the oil business but trusted his abilities and knowledge to make informed decisions. When ventures failed, he moved forward without dwelling on disappointment.

His vision extended beyond business success to creating meaningful impact for his community. He chose his mindset and actions daily, maintaining energy and optimism even when the path forward seemed unclear. This steadfast outlook became contagious, inspiring those around him to approach challenges with the same resilient spirit.

Optimism rooted in action turns hope into momentum.

Standing on Principle: The Courage to Fight for What's Right

My father's resilience was perhaps most evident in his willingness to stand firm on principle, regardless of the personal cost. Two significant legal battles demonstrate this commitment—fights he undertook not because winning was guaranteed, but because the cause was just.

When the federal government passed the Natural Gas Policy Act of 1978 (NGPA), my father saw it as fundamentally unfair and unconstitutional. The law gave federal authorities control over intrastate gas that was produced, sold, and consumed entirely within state boundaries. As a believer in states' rights, he viewed this as government overreach that gave pipeline companies too much power, especially over small producers.

He began building support for a legal challenge, reaching out to state officials across natural gas-producing regions. While many agreed with his position in principle, they backed away when it came to funding the lawsuit. The political and financial risks were too great. Undeterred, my father used his own resources to finance the battle.

Several states, including Oklahoma, Texas, and Louisiana, eventually joined as plaintiffs in federal court. When the judge ruled against them, my father funded an appeal to the Tenth Circuit Court of Appeals, and ultimately to the U.S. Supreme Court. Though he lost at every level, he never regretted the fight. He had stood up for what he believed was right, regardless of the outcome.

This same principled approach guided him in a case that would have a far-reaching impact. While reviewing data from wells in Garfield

County, Oklahoma, he noticed something troubling: a small gas well in Section 4 was barely producing, despite being surrounded by highly productive wells owned by several major oil companies. Further investigation revealed these companies were draining gas from under Section 4 without drilling the replacement well they were obligated to provide.

This discovery led him to Sarah Spaeth, an elderly widow who held the mineral rights in Section 4. Recognizing that she was being taken advantage of, my father offered to fight on her behalf if she would grant his company a top lease. He promised that she could keep any damages awarded, while he would cover all legal expenses.

The oil companies fought relentlessly. When the Oklahoma Corporation Commission denied his initial application, my father appealed to the Oklahoma Supreme Court. After winning that appeal but still facing opposition, he helped Mrs. Spaeth file a lawsuit that would stretch across eight years and multiple courts.

Finally, in 1982, a federal jury found that Union Oil had acted fraudulently and breached its duty to Mrs. Spaeth. She was awarded substantial damages—$22,807 in actual damages and initially $3 million in punitive damages (later reduced to $2 million). The case established a new legal precedent for "fraudulent drainage" that would protect countless mineral owners in the future.

On the day Union finally transferred the money, my father simply nodded and said, "We got there. We were in the right." He didn't mention the years of work or what it had cost him. The victory wasn't about personal gain—it was about justice for someone who couldn't fight for herself.

Legacy isn't built on winning every battle. It's built on choosing battles that matter and standing firm no matter the outcome.

Keeping the Team Together Through Crisis

One of my father's greatest strengths was his ability to maintain team cohesion during dire circumstances. He never sugarcoated challenges or hid harsh realities. Instead, he combined honesty with vision, ensuring everyone understood both the struggles ahead and their crucial role in overcoming them.

A pivotal moment came when the company was barely staying afloat. Revenue had dried up, and there wasn't enough money to cover payroll. Two senior leaders returned from visiting field workers with a grim assessment: there was no path forward except bankruptcy and closure.

My father listened to their conclusion, then responded with quiet certainty: "You know, sometimes you make decisions about money that aren't about the money." He refused to accept defeat, promising that everyone would be paid, the business would continue, and they would find a path to new growth.

What his employees didn't know was that he was using his personal royalty income to keep the company afloat, covering salaries and expenses from his own pocket. He had a deep connection to the field workers—having started his career as a roughneck in the oilfields to pay for college—and felt a personal responsibility to them and their families.

By sheer force of will and unwavering belief in the business and its people, he guided the company through this dark period. His optimism became contagious, fueling the team's resilience. He didn't just keep the company alive—he brought it back stronger, proving that with enough determination, any challenge could be overcome.

Leadership is at its most powerful when it carries others through storms they cannot yet see the end of.

Conclusion: The Legacy of Resilience

My father's life demonstrates the transformative power of resilience. From early business struggles to industry downturns, legal battles, and financial crises, his ability to persevere in the face of adversity defined his leadership. His optimism, innovative thinking, principled stands, and commitment to his team weren't just qualities that helped him succeed—they were the foundation of his legacy.

The setbacks he faced weren't roadblocks; they were opportunities for growth. His resilience and single-minded determination allowed him to sustain his journey through challenges that would have defeated most others. His story reminds us that true leadership isn't about avoiding failure—it's about rising above it, transforming obstacles into stepping stones toward a greater purpose.

Chapter 5

A Beacon for Others: How One Life Can Light the Way for Many

> "Leadership is not about being in charge. It's about taking care of those in your charge."
> —Simon Sinek

From Personal Resilience to Collective Impact

The journey of resilience my father traveled wasn't solely for his own benefit. Each challenge he overcame, each obstacle he pushed through, built not only his character but also his capacity to lift others. The true measure of his leadership wasn't found in personal achievements but in how his strength became a foundation upon which others could build their own success.

While Chapter 4 explored how my father sustained his own journey through adversity, this chapter examines how his resilience transformed into a beacon that guided others. His leadership wasn't about position or authority—it was about presence, influence, and the ability to inspire those around him to reach heights they might never have attempted alone.

Leading with Conviction and Care

My father had a way of filling a room without raising his voice. It wasn't just presence; it was the deep conviction he carried into every conversation, every decision. When he spoke, you could feel that he wasn't guessing. He believed fully in what he stood for: family, faith, hard work, and truth.

People trusted him because he was consistent. He didn't sell ideas. He lived them. Whether negotiating tough oil deals, walking a school campus he helped save, or sitting quietly beside a scared young racer at a dusty track, he was the same man. His confidence didn't come from being the loudest; it came from being the surest about what mattered most.

In a world that often rewards noise and flash, my father showed that real leadership comes from steady, stubborn conviction and from caring more about people than appearances.

Building Loyalty One Life at a Time

The loyalty my father inspired wasn't because of his title or position. It was personal. He built it one conversation, one risk, one act of belief at a time.

One of the clearest memories I have of this was when fear and love collided at a local racetrack.

When Fear and Love Sit in the Same Lawn Chair

From the time my son was old enough to pick up a toy, he chose cars. He lined them up in rows like a NASCAR starting grid, moving them around the carpet with leader changes, pit stops, crashes, and winners. Before he could speak in full sentences, he could name drivers, sponsors, and car numbers from memory. Racing wasn't something he liked. It was part of who he was.

Our family attended a conservative Christian church that taught that drinking alcohol was wrong. My son loved the sport so much that he wore his Budweiser NASCAR shirt to Sunday service without a second thought. Nobody could miss the passion in him.

What made it more complicated was that he had been diagnosed with Cystic Fibrosis as an infant. His days were shaped by special diets, treatments, and medical appointments. There was no cure. Every choice we made for him pointed toward the same goal: keep him healthy, keep him here.

One evening when he was eight years old, a family friend invited us to a local dirt track. It wasn't the polished world of NASCAR. It was loud, dirty, and smelled of race fuel. We stood by the fence all night, breathing it in. I could see it clearly: my son wasn't just watching. He was trying to belong.

During the evening, we learned about a car that was coming available—a real starter car for young racers. When I asked if he would be interested, he lit up in a way I hadn't seen before.

I wanted to say yes. But fear pulled at me. We had no experience in racing. No safety net. No idea what this would mean for his health. What if the dust and fumes damaged his lungs? What if he got hurt? Would we be giving him something he loved, or would we be taking away the life we had fought so hard to protect?

My wife and I talked for a long time that night. In the end, we agreed: the greater risk was standing still. If we waited for a time when it would feel completely safe, we might wait forever. Better to let him chase his passion now than wonder later what might have been.

Still, it wasn't a decision we could carry alone. I went to my father. I told him everything: the risks, the cost, the unknowns. I told him how much I wanted to say yes, and how much it scared me. He listened. He asked hard questions. He admitted he was afraid. He didn't want to see his grandson injured. He didn't want to see his lungs worsen because of race fumes and dirt. And yet, even in his fear, he said yes. He gave sponsorship money. He showed up. He and my mother sat by the fence in their lawn chairs at every race, cheering on my son, whether he finished first or last.

In the early years, there weren't many trophies. There were more spins and setbacks than celebrations. But we kept learning. And over time, success came. Through it all, my father never wavered. He invested even when he was afraid. He believed in something bigger than safety. He believed in letting his grandson live.

This is one of the clearest pictures I have of the kind of man he was: Someone who gave even when it scared him. Someone who chose love over fear.

He believed in people before they fully believed in themselves.

He took that same approach with his employees. He walked the floors. He asked about their families. He noticed the quiet ones, the struggling ones. He didn't separate leadership from friendship. He knew they were made of the same material: trust, consistency, presence.

Creating Space for Others to Grow

Leadership, for my father, wasn't about taking the spotlight. It was about making room for others to shine.

When my mother wanted to go back to school, it would have been easy for him to say it wasn't practical. Money was tight. Time was even tighter. Instead, he rearranged his schedule. He watched us kids. He shouldered more work at home. He wanted her to have the space to chase her dream the way he had chased his.

Later, when she bought a travel agency with friends, my father didn't just cheer from the sidelines. He helped fund it. He stood beside her. He believed that leadership wasn't about demanding loyalty. It was about earning it by believing in the dreams of others, not just your own.

Their story is one I'll never forget. He showed me that the real measure of a leader isn't how many people follow you, it's how many people grow because you're there.

Ralph and Maxine visiting Ralph's parents. They were in college and dating.

Leading with Truth, Especially When It Costs You

My mother was creative, intelligent, and determined. She finished her college degree in education in just three years while my father prepared for graduate school. When they moved to Oklahoma City, she began her career as an elementary school teacher. She loved the work. She loved connecting with her students, encouraging them, and watching them discover what they could do.

Early in their marriage, life kept moving faster than they expected. My father's first jobs in the oil and gas industry required them to relocate several times. When they eventually returned to Oklahoma to start a family, they had already weathered instability, financial strain, and long seasons of uncertainty.

When I was born, they faced a hard reality. My mother's teaching salary barely covered the cost of childcare, and my father's career was still unpredictable. There were seasons when the mortgage didn't get paid. They wanted to be independent from their parents and to stand on their own, but survival often felt like the greater achievement.

After long conversations and difficult prayers, they decided my mother would leave her teaching career to care for me full-time. They would live on what my father could earn, trusting that somehow it would be enough. It was a risk they were willing to take together.

My mother threw herself into that life. She became a leader among the parents at my school, organizing support and building community. When my sister was born, she expanded her influence even further, pouring herself into our home, our schools, and the lives around her.

Even so, her drive to grow and contribute never disappeared. When the time was right, she decided to pursue graduate school.

Making that possible was no small thing. Money was still tight. Time was precious. Raising two children while earning a graduate degree required sacrifice from everyone.

My father made sure she had what she needed to succeed. He arranged his schedule so he could care for us when she needed time to study. He took on more responsibilities at home. Together, they stretched every dollar to cover tuition, bills, and groceries.

The day my mother graduated, I can still picture the pride on both their faces. It belonged to both of them.

Even after all that work, she once again chose to put her professional ambitions on hold. The cost of pursuing two full careers, with two young children at home, was too great. They made another sacrifice together, placing our future ahead of their own.

She held on to her gifts and waited.

Years later, when my sister and I were older and my father's business had found its footing, an opportunity came. A small travel agency was for sale. My mother and a few close friends decided to buy it. None of them had experience in the travel industry, but they knew how to lead, how to build relationships, and how to create value.

My father supported her fully. He helped finance the purchase. He encouraged the risk. He stood beside her, just as she had once stood beside him.

At first, the agency struggled. Then, a partnership opportunity opened with a major airline, focusing on international missionary travel. The business grew, reaching clients around the world. It became a thriving success, built on the same creativity and determination that had marked my mother's life from the beginning.

Her professional success was real and lasting. More than that, it was proof—to herself and to all of us—that her dreams had never been wasted. They had simply been waiting for their time. My father celebrated her every step of the way.

This is the kind of leader he was. He believed in sacrifice, but not in silencing dreams. He created space for the people he loved to find fulfillment in their own time, in their own way. He led not by commanding attention, but by standing steady beside those he believed in most.

When my mother's moment came, he wasn't ahead of her or behind her. He was right there, leading from beside her.

There were times when leadership cost him.

When a university board he served on tried to profit off land meant for future students, he pushed back. He gathered every document, rebuilt the full timeline, and made his case. They dismissed him from the board. He lost influence and position, but he didn't lose himself.

Even after that, he continued to quietly support the university financially. He refused to let disappointment harden his heart. Leadership wasn't about winning. It was about staying faithful to what was right, no matter who was watching.

And when it came time to honor the people who had poured into his own life, he led with quiet, steady generosity.

Honoring Sacrifice and Restoring What Was Lost

In the early years of our family, my father often felt the weight of expectation from his own parents. There was a time when my grandfather urged him to give up the uncertainty of the oil and gas business and find stable work that would guarantee a steady income. My father understood the concern, but he was determined to build something different. He used to say, "You can lead me a little, but you can't push me."

Through those years of instability—lost jobs, unpaid mortgages, and the daily strain of raising a young family—my father received little practical support from my grandfather. He carried the burden himself, holding tightly to the belief that perseverance would one day bear fruit.

In 1972, everything changed for my grandfather. The company he had worked for closed its local operations, and with it, he lost not only his job but also the retirement income he had counted on. Because of the strict eligibility rules in place at the time, many employees, including my grandfather, were denied the pensions they had spent their lives working toward.

For a man who had built his identity on finishing every job, honoring every commitment, and trusting others to do the same, the loss was devastating. He felt betrayed. The promises he had kept to others had not been kept to him.

At the same time, my father was beginning to find real success. Marlin Oil was no longer just an idea—it was becoming a thriving company. He saw the fear and grief in his father's eyes. He understood the depth of the loss: not just financial, but personal.

My father decided to act. He wanted to honor the sacrifices his parents had made for him, the values they had instilled, the quiet lessons they had lived. He didn't want to make them feel dependent. He wanted to restore something that had been unfairly taken.

He chose to give them a share in one of his profitable oil wells. It became their own property, a source of income that allowed them to live with dignity and independence. It wasn't a handout. It was an acknowledgment, a way of saying, "Your life's work mattered. It still matters."

Through that simple but profound act, my father showed a different kind of leadership. The kind that recognizes sacrifice, restores honor, and quietly offers back what the world has stolen. The kind that leads by building others up, even when no one is looking.

A Legacy of Presence and Perseverance

In the end, my father's leadership didn't look like grand speeches or sweeping strategies. It looked like a man who sat by the track, who stayed up late helping his wife study, who guaranteed a school's bonds with his own future, who believed a young man deserved another shot when the world said he didn't.

It looked like someone who knew that fear and love often sit in the same lawn chair—and who chose love every time.

His leadership taught me that real success isn't measured in what you build. It's measured in who you build up.

And it taught me that the greatest leaders aren't the ones who light their own way the brightest.

They're the ones who become a beacon so others can find their way, too.

Chapter 6

A Legacy in the Making: The Long-Term Impact of Determined Leadership

"The true meaning of life is to plant trees, under whose shade you do not expect to sit."
—Nelson Henderson

Teaching His Children Grit and Compassion

For my father, the greatest legacy one could leave wasn't about wealth or achievements. It was the values passed on to the next generation. Grit and compassion weren't just concepts he talked about; they were lessons he lived out, and he made sure my sister and I experienced them firsthand.

Growing up, he often reminded us, "Life won't always be easy, but the hard times will make you stronger." He demonstrated this by pushing us into situations that required perseverance, from summer jobs to personal challenges. He knew that growth only came from hard work and persistence. Yet, despite this toughness, he balanced it with a remarkable sense of compassion. He taught us that strength meant little if it wasn't accompanied by kindness. He frequently said, "Success means nothing if it's not used to help others." That dual focus on resilience and empathy shaped how we approached our own lives.

We've tried to pass down these same values to our children. We've encouraged them to face obstacles with courage and determination. All three have participated in sports, pursued their education with focus, and taken on challenges that required grit. For our two children with cystic fibrosis, managing a chronic illness has added another layer of difficulty, but they have faced it head-on. They have refused to let it limit their potential, choosing instead to pursue excellence and embrace life's possibilities with resilience and optimism.

My father's teaching wasn't confined to lectures; he led by example. Whenever we faced a tough situation, he was there to support us, but he never solved our problems for us. Instead, he gave us the tools we needed to overcome challenges on our own, fostering a deep sense of self-reliance and empathy for others.

One personal story that stands out was when I called him during my surgery internship in New York City. I was exhausted, mentally and physically drained, and began questioning whether I had made the right choice to become a physician. I even considered switching careers to law. My father didn't lecture me or give me an easy way out. Instead, he calmly said, "Mark, I think you should do whatever you think you can afford to do." In that one simple statement, he handed the responsibility back to me. It was a turning point in my life, and I now realize that his confidence in my ability to navigate my own challenges gave me the strength to continue on my path.

Legacy is defined by the qualities and values that are handed down to future generations, rather than by awards or achievements.

This is me with my father, taken around 1961, during a time when he had been laid off and was struggling to provide for our family while trying to advance in his career. Despite these challenges, he remained optimistic and happy. This was taken at home.

Modeling Work Ethic and Perseverance

If my father had a superpower, it was his tireless work ethic and relentless perseverance. He taught us that success didn't come from shortcuts but from showing up every day, being ready to work hard, and doing your best. He lived this lesson, especially during times of uncertainty in his business or personal challenges.

After earning his master's degree in geology, my father began working for Shell Oil Company. But in 1960, during an oil bust, Shell laid off about a third of its geological staff, including my father. With little savings and a family to support, he found himself in an incredibly tough situation. Instead of giving up, he spent his days at the Oklahoma City Geological Library, tirelessly mapping out new oil prospects. He had an incredible talent for identifying unexplored opportunities and pitched his prospects to potential investors, even though the industry was struggling and buyers were few.

Despite these challenges, my father kept moving forward. Things got so tight that my mother had to ask the butcher for bones "for the dogs" to make soup, even though we didn't have any dogs. My parents were on the verge of losing their home. Yet, my father kept a spring in his step and a smile on his face, determined to find a way through.

When he finally pitched a promising deal to a local independent petroleum company, they liked it but only offered him a percentage of future production with no up-front cash. Knowing that he needed money immediately to avoid foreclosure on our home, my father made a bold move. He folded up his maps, smiled, and said, "I need $1,500 in cash, even if it means I don't get a share of the well." The company's leader relented, and that check stopped the foreclosure. One by one, my father's prospects proved profitable, and in 1972, he founded Marlin Oil Corporation. That perseverance, pushing forward when everything seemed bleak, was the cornerstone of his success.

The Birth of Marlin Oil: A Dream Ten Years in the Making

During that challenging period, my father found support through close friendships. One evening, exhausted from another day of searching for work and stability, he sat with a friend who was an artist and designer. As they talked late into the night, my father shared his ultimate dream—not just finding oil for others, but building his own company where he could fully apply his geological vision and leadership principles.

The conversation turned to what he might name this future company. My father wanted something deeply personal that reflected what mattered most to him—his family. Together, they conceived the idea of combining my name, Mark, with my sister's middle name, Lynn. From this simple combination, "Marlin Oil" was born.

His friend even sketched a logo depicting a marlin fish leaping over an offshore drilling rig—a visual embodiment of ambition and energy that perfectly captured my father's vision. Though it would take a decade for this dream to materialize, that conversation planted a seed that my father nurtured through years of continued struggle and gradual progress.

The name and logo became more than branding elements—they were daily reminders of why he persisted through setbacks. Every time he faced a new challenge, the name "Marlin" reconnected him to his core purpose. He wasn't just building a business; he was creating a legacy for his children, whose very names were woven into the enterprise.

When he finally founded Marlin Oil Corporation in 1972, it represented not just a business achievement but the culmination of a journey sustained by unwavering vision. What others might have seen as merely a corporate identity was, for my father, the embodiment of his deepest values—family, perseverance, and the determination to build something meaningful that would outlast him.

The company grew to become exactly what he had envisioned that night years earlier—a platform for applying his unique geological insights and leadership principles. It became the foundation for his broader impact, enabling the philanthropy and community investment that would define his later years. Most importantly, it remained a family enterprise in both name and spirit, with the values that inspired its creation continuing to guide its operations long after its founding.

Perseverance isn't about having a perfect path; it's about showing up, standing firm, and believing in the next step even when it's hard to see.

Directing Resources to Others' Education

Education was one of the causes closest to my father's heart. He believed that empowering young people through education was one of the most profound ways to create lasting change. Over the years, he dedicated significant resources to ensure that deserving students had access to higher education.

For my father, education wasn't just about paying tuition; it was about helping individuals build their future. He took an active role in the lives of the students he supported, offering mentorship and guidance. He believed in nurturing the whole person, not just providing financial aid. He regularly met with students, offering advice and encouragement, reinforcing that education was the foundation for achieving their full potential.

Investing in education was a way to invest in a future that he would never fully see, built because he believed in it.

Supporting Youth and Educational Institutions

Beyond individual students, my father was deeply committed to creating opportunities for young people. His work with children's homes and educational institutions was a way to lift up those who needed it most.

From as early as I can remember, my father was drawn to children in difficult situations. Through our church, he got involved with children's homes—places where orphaned kids or those from families in crisis could find safety and support. Back then, there were few resources for these kids, and my father believed they needed more than just shelter. They needed encouragement, a reminder that they mattered.

Growing up, we often had kids from these homes over for holidays. My father stayed connected with them throughout his life. As he became more successful, he did not forget about the challenges they faced. He wanted to do something meaningful for them, and Christmas became a way to do that.

These kids rarely had the chance to ask for something they wanted. They were used to being told what they needed, such as food, clothes, or school supplies. My father wanted them to experience something different, so he reached out to two children's homes in Oklahoma and asked the kids to write letters telling him what they really wanted for Christmas.

For years, this became a tradition. The letters would come back with requests for sporting equipment, bikes, and music players, things most kids take for granted but that were out of reach for them. My father believed it was important for them to ask for something they truly wanted, something that someone could say yes to, something that would become their own.

When I got older, I had the chance to join my parents in delivering these gifts. Seeing the kids' excitement made it clear how much this meant to them. But what stood out most was how much it meant to my father. He was grateful for the chance to bring them joy, even for a moment. Encouragement was at the heart of everything he did, and this was his way of showing these kids they were seen and valued.

He never did it for recognition. He did not want awards or his name on a plaque. He did it year after year because he cared.

Encouragement given at the right moment can alter the entire course of a young person's life.

A Quiet Investment in Someone Else's Dream

My father was always reading. The newspaper was never just news to him. It was a window into the lives of people fighting their own battles, building their futures, pushing through obstacles that would stop most others.

One day, as he scanned the pages like he always did, he found a story that made him pause. It was about a high school girl in western Oklahoma. She was a standout basketball player, competing and excelling at a level most players only dreamed about. But what made her story different, what would have captured my father's full attention, was that she was doing it all while deaf.

Where others might have seen her success as unlikely or even impossible, my father would have seen something else entirely. He would have felt pure joy. Pride, too. Because perseverance, the refusal to be defined by limits, was a language he understood deeply.

As he read further, he learned something that unsettled him. Despite her achievements, she wasn't planning to pursue basketball in college. She believed her deafness would hold her back. It wasn't a lack of skill or work ethic. It was a barrier that had been placed in her path—a barrier of circumstance and of cost.

For my father, that kind of barrier was never acceptable. He quietly had his team reach out to her family. He learned she was a candidate for a cochlear implant, something that could open doors she hadn't even dared to imagine. But the cost was overwhelming, and her family simply couldn't afford it.

My father didn't hesitate. With the family's support and the student's excitement and determination, he made the decision. He covered the medical bills. He made the cochlear implant possible.

The surgery was a success. And for the first time, she wasn't limited by her deafness. She could dream dreams that had once felt too far out of reach. College athletics were back on the table. A whole new life opened before her.

My father never told anyone about it. He didn't want recognition. Even many people close to him had no idea it ever happened. He simply saw someone fighting to succeed and stepped in quietly, faithfully, to make sure the next chapter of her story could be written with possibility, not limitation.

He believed that belief itself was an investment. And sometimes, the greatest leadership happens not in the spotlight, but in the quiet spaces where one dream meets one open hand.

Conclusion: A Legacy of Empowerment

My father's legacy is one of grit, compassion, and unwavering belief in the potential of others. Through his example, he taught us the importance of hard work and perseverance, balanced by empathy and kindness. His contributions to education and mentorship left an indelible mark on his community and the lives of countless young people. More than anything, his ability to see and cultivate potential in others ensured that his legacy of determined leadership would continue for generations to come.

The greatest leaders plant seeds they may never see grow, trusting that the harvest will be even greater than they imagined.

Ralph during his college years at the University of Oklahoma

Conclusion

A Legacy of Values: Tools for Building a Life of Purpose and Impact

As we look back on my father's life, it becomes clear that his success wasn't just built on business acumen or hard work. His success was built on a foundation of values that guided every decision he made. These values are now the bedrock of our family, our business, and our philanthropy. They serve as a compass, guiding us toward a future filled with purpose, integrity, and collaboration.

To lead with clarity, conviction, and impact, we must keep these values at the center of everything we do. For our family, our team, our partners, and future generations, alignment with these values is not just important. Alignment is essential. What follows isn't just a reflection on my father's legacy. It's a toolbox for leaders, collaborators, and future generations to take these principles and build something extraordinary.

The lessons my father lived by can serve as a guide for anyone seeking to lead with purpose. A life rooted in values leaves a mark far deeper than any single achievement ever could.

Here are the key principles that defined his success and can shape yours.

TOOL 1: SINGLE-MINDED VISION

MY FATHER BELIEVED DEEPLY IN THE POWER OF VISION. HE DIDN'T JUST SEE THE FUTURE AS IT WAS; HE SAW IT AS IT COULD BE. HIS UNWAVERING FOCUS ON HIS GOALS ALLOWED HIM TO PUSH THROUGH CHALLENGES THAT WOULD HAVE STOPPED OTHERS. BUT HIS SINGLE-MINDEDNESS WASN'T BLIND AMBITION. HIS AMBITION WAS A PURPOSEFUL PURSUIT OF SOMETHING GREATER.

Vision without steadfastness fades. It's the daily commitment to that vision that builds a lasting legacy.

HOW TO USE IT:

DEFINE YOUR NORTH STAR: BE CLEAR ABOUT YOUR LONG-TERM GOALS, BOTH PERSONALLY AND PROFESSIONALLY. WHAT'S THE BIGGER PICTURE YOU'RE WORKING TOWARD? WRITE IT DOWN, REVISIT IT REGULARLY, AND LET IT GUIDE YOU THROUGH TOUGH TIMES.

MAKE DECISIONS WITH PURPOSE: WHEN FACED WITH DIFFICULT CHOICES, ASK YOURSELF, "DOES THIS ALIGN WITH MY VISION?" IF IT DOESN'T, HAVE THE COURAGE TO WALK AWAY, EVEN WHEN IT'S HARD.

COMMUNICATE YOUR VISION: WHETHER YOU'RE LEADING A TEAM OR COLLABORATING WITH PARTNERS, ENSURE EVERYONE UNDERSTANDS AND SHARES THE VISION. A COMMON PURPOSE UNITES AND MOTIVATES, ESPECIALLY IN CHALLENGING MOMENTS.

TOOL 2: RESILIENCE IN THE FACE OF ADVERSITY

IF THERE'S ONE VALUE THAT DEFINED MY FATHER'S LIFE, IT WAS RESILIENCE. HE FACED HEALTH CHALLENGES, BUSINESS SETBACKS, AND EVEN BETRAYAL, BUT HE NEVER WAVERED. TO HIM, SUCCESS WASN'T ABOUT AVOIDING FAILURE; IT WAS ABOUT RISING ABOVE IT.

Resilience transforms obstacles from reasons to quit into reasons to rise higher.

HOW TO USE IT:

EMBRACE SETBACKS AS OPPORTUNITIES: EVERY CHALLENGE IS A CHANCE TO LEARN. WHEN ADVERSITY STRIKES, ASK YOURSELF, "WHAT CAN I LEARN FROM THIS? HOW WILL THIS MAKE ME STRONGER?"

MAINTAIN OPTIMISM: DIFFICULT TIMES ARE INEVITABLE, BUT YOUR RESPONSE MAKES ALL THE DIFFERENCE. STAY FOCUSED ON THE FUTURE, KNOWING THAT PERSEVERANCE WILL CARRY YOU THROUGH.

SUPPORT OTHERS THROUGH ADVERSITY: RESILIENCE ISN'T JUST ABOUT PERSONAL STRENGTH; IT'S ABOUT HELPING OTHERS STAY STRONG. BE THERE FOR YOUR TEAM, YOUR FAMILY, AND YOUR PARTNERS WHEN THEY NEED SUPPORT AND ENCOURAGEMENT.

TOOL 3: PASSION WITH PURPOSE

MY FATHER HAD A COMPETITIVE FIRE, BUT HIS PASSION WAS ALWAYS GUIDED BY A HIGHER PURPOSE. WHETHER HE WAS COMPETING ON THE BASEBALL FIELD OR IN THE BOARDROOM, IT WASN'T JUST ABOUT WINNING. COMPETITION WAS ABOUT MAKING A DIFFERENCE AND PUSHING BOUNDARIES TO CREATE A LASTING IMPACT.

Purpose gives passion direction and turns effort into enduring impact.

HOW TO USE IT:

CHANNEL YOUR PASSION: PASSION BY ITSELF ISN'T ENOUGH. ASK YOURSELF, "WHAT'S THE PURPOSE BEHIND MY PASSION? HOW CAN I USE MY DRIVE TO CREATE SOMETHING MEANINGFUL?"

LEAD WITH CONVICTION: WHEN YOU BELIEVE DEEPLY IN WHAT YOU'RE DOING, OTHERS WILL FOLLOW. SHOW YOUR TEAM AND PARTNERS THAT YOUR EFFORTS ARE ABOUT MORE THAN JUST SUCCESS. THEY'RE ABOUT PURPOSE.

INSPIRE THROUGH ACTION: PASSION ISN'T JUST ABOUT WORDS; IT'S ABOUT ACTION. BE THE FIRST TO STEP UP WHEN TIMES ARE TOUGH AND LEAD BY EXAMPLE. YOUR COMMITMENT WILL INSPIRE OTHERS.

TOOL 4: FAITH AND GENEROSITY

FAITH WAS AT THE CORE OF MY FATHER'S LIFE, SHAPING NOT JUST HIS PERSONAL BELIEFS BUT HIS APPROACH TO BUSINESS. HE BELIEVED IN GIVING SACRIFICIALLY, SUPPORTING OTHERS, AND INVESTING IN CAUSES THAT ALIGNED WITH HIS VALUES. HIS GENEROSITY WAS AN EXTENSION OF HIS FAITH, A BELIEF IN THE GREATER GOOD, AND IN USING HIS RESOURCES TO MAKE A DIFFERENCE.

True generosity isn't measured by the size of the gift, but by the heart behind it.

HOW TO USE IT:

GIVE PURPOSEFULLY: WHETHER IN BUSINESS OR PHILANTHROPY, BE INTENTIONAL ABOUT WHERE YOU DIRECT YOUR RESOURCES. SUPPORT CAUSES THAT ALIGN WITH YOUR VALUES AND HAVE THE POTENTIAL FOR LASTING IMPACT.

LEAD WITH INTEGRITY: FAITH AND ETHICS GO HAND IN HAND. MAKE SURE EVERY DECISION REFLECTS YOUR VALUES, EVEN WHEN NO ONE IS WATCHING.

INVEST IN PEOPLE: GENEROSITY ISN'T JUST FINANCIAL. INVEST TIME, ENERGY, AND BELIEF IN OTHERS. HELP THEM GROW, MENTOR THOSE AROUND YOU, AND LIFT THEM UP TO REACH THEIR POTENTIAL.

TOOL 5: BUILDING A COMMUNITY OF BELIEVERS AND DOERS

MY FATHER UNDERSTOOD THAT NO LEADER SUCCEEDS ALONE. HE SURROUNDED HIMSELF WITH PEOPLE WHO BELIEVED IN HIS VISION, SHARED HIS VALUES, AND WERE WILLING TO WORK TOWARD A COMMON GOAL. HE BUILT A COMMUNITY OF BELIEVERS AND DOERS, PEOPLE COMMITTED TO TURNING IDEAS INTO ACTION.

A great leader builds not just companies, but communities where belief turns into shared action.

HOW TO USE IT:

SURROUND YOURSELF WITH THE RIGHT PEOPLE: CHOOSE YOUR COLLABORATORS, PARTNERS, AND TEAM MEMBERS CAREFULLY. LOOK FOR THOSE WHO SHARE YOUR VALUES AND ALIGN WITH YOUR VISION.

CREATE A CULTURE OF ACCOUNTABILITY: IN ANY PARTNERSHIP OR TEAM, ACCOUNTABILITY IS VITAL. MAKE SURE EVERYONE IS COMMITTED NOT ONLY TO THEIR SUCCESS BUT TO THE SUCCESS OF THE WHOLE.

FOSTER COLLABORATION: GREAT IDEAS OFTEN COME FROM COLLABORATION. ENCOURAGE OPEN DIALOGUE, CREATIVE THINKING, AND THE SHARING OF IDEAS. WHEN EVERYONE WORKS TOWARD THE SAME PURPOSE, THE RESULTS WILL FOLLOW.

A Final Word of Gratitude

As I carry my father's legacy forward, I'm filled with gratitude for the lessons he taught me, the values he lived by, and the opportunity to share those values with all of you. Our family and business are built on these principles, and they continue to guide us as we grow, collaborate, and impact the world.

To those who walk this journey with us, our team, partners, advisors, and collaborators—thank you for believing in these values as we do. Together, we can create something lasting, meaningful, and truly reflective of the legacy of determined leadership.

This is the way forward. With vision, resilience, passion, faith, and community, we can build a future that honors the past and paves the way for future generations.

Leadership that lasts is not about monuments or medals. It is the simple, faithful work of planting seeds and trusting that the harvest will bless generations we may never meet.

Legacy is not what we leave for people. Legacy is what we leave within them: belief, resilience, vision, and heart.

Carrying the Legacy Forward

Mark N. Harvey, M.D., is a cardiologist specializing in cardiac electrophysiology at the Oklahoma Heart Hospital in Oklahoma City. With more than 30 years of experience, he has dedicated his career to advancing patient care through both precision and compassion.

Beyond the hospital walls, Dr. Harvey leads the Harvey Family Foundation, based in Edmond, Oklahoma. The foundation invests in scientific research, education, and community initiatives. It extends the values of resilience, generosity, and service that shaped his upbringing.

This book is a reflection of the lessons Dr. Harvey learned from his greatest mentor, his father, Ralph Harvey. Through decades of professional practice and philanthropy, Dr. Harvey has seen firsthand that true leadership is not measured by titles or success alone. It is measured by the lives we impact, the values we uphold, and the legacy we leave behind.

In sharing his family's story, Dr. Harvey invites readers into a vision of leadership rooted in conviction, care, and the quiet strength to keep going when others might quit. His life's work in medicine, community, and now in writing is a continuation of the determined leadership he was blessed to witness and carry forward.

www.harveyff.org

www.ingramcontent.com/pod-product-compliance
Lightning Source LLC
Chambersburg PA
CBHW052205070526
44585CB00017B/2070